STEAM COLOUR PORTFOLIO

SOUTHERN REGION
Volume One

Keith R.Pirt

BOOK LAW PUBLICATIONS

First published in the United Kingdom by Book Law Publications 2005
382 Carlton Hill, Nottingham, NG4 1JA
Printed and bound by The Amadeus Press, Cleckheaton, West Yorkshire.

Introduction

When Keith Pirt passed away earlier this year many people feared that his negative and transparency collection would be lost, either consigned to a rubbish skip, as has been the fate of many previous large and small photographic collections, or that it would be purchased for a private collection never to be seen again by the public or his many friends. As luck would have it, Keith had set up a contract in 2004 with Book Law Publications to have much of his work published in landscape format so that each picture could be shown to its best advantage. Alas, he only saw the first two introductory volumes published before his demise.

However, his family realised the value of the collection to the railway fraternity and passed on their wishes to the publisher that they would like to see the bulk of the planned series come to fruition as Keith would have wanted. Therefore, this particular volume can be counted as the first to feature solely the locomotives of the Southern Region.

The reason why the Southern has been chosen as the first of many such albums which will show off Keith's 'slides' to their best, is because KRP took his annual holidays 'down south' to places where he could not normally reach at weekends or during the long summer evenings after work. Basically, Keith loved his trips to the southern and south-western counties of England not just because of the railway lure but also because he looked upon nature's contribution to the countryside with a keen naturalists eye. Many of the locations where he set up his camera had more than just a train in view; the beautiful rolling countryside would also get into the picture by design. So, we are sure that KRP would have approved of our choice for the first solo volume; it gave him many happy memories and as a result he gave us a harvest of excellent colour photography to marvel.

Roger Griffiths wrote the captions for which the publisher is most grateful. The captions are somewhat longer than what Keith would have provided as he was a man who believed in the maxim that "...a picture paints a thousand words...". However, we, like most railway enthusiasts like as many words as possible to accompany featured pictures, so we have combined the two and hope that you like the mix.

Similarly, the pictures within the album are arranged in a mixed, rather than themed, presentation. Main line scenes face branch line tranquillity, streamlined 'namers' meet black liveried tank engines. Enjoy the nostalgia, the atmosphere and the gone forever everyday scenes of yesteryear.

There are many more volumes to come in this landscape format series. The LMS, LNER, BR Standards, Diesels, Irish and overseas railways, oh! and the GWR types will all be presented in superb colour nor will Keith's extensive black and white collection, which dates from the early 1950s, be overlooked, it is also hoped to publish a number of books in this ever-popular format. All will be shown exactly as captured by one of Britain's premier railway photographers - the late Keith R. Pirt.

David Allen, Nottingham, October 2005.

'Merchant Navy' No.35003 ROYAL MAIL is here seen between Basingstoke and Worting Junction with a Down West of England express in September 1963. Entering traffic on 13th September 1941 as No.21C3, the engine was named six weeks later at Waterloo station, by Lord Essendon, the Chairman of Royal Mail Lines. The locomotive was given black livery in May 1943, reverting to Malachite green in November 1945. Rebuilding came in August 1959 along with class doyen 35001 CHANNEL PACKET, these being almost the last engines of the class to be altered (35006 and 35028 being the last, in October 1959). Withdrawal of No.35003 came in July 1967 with the end of steam on the Southern Region. The engine had amassed a total of 1,131,793 miles in traffic. Stored at Nine Elms until about October 1967, No.35003 was hauled to the Newport, South Wales scrapyard of G.Cashmore, where cutting up occurred in December the same year. British Railways shed allocations: Exmouth Junction; June 1964 Nine Elms; August 1964 Bournemouth; October 1966 Weymouth; March 1967 Nine Elms.

The Royal Mail Steam Packet Company started running mails to the West Indies in 1841. Years of expansion followed until a disastrous financial collapse in 1932, from which Royal Mail Lines Ltd emerged. Absorbed by Furness, Withy & Company in 1965, Royal Mail Lines virtually ceased to exist by 1972. *(BLP - S20)*

A rare picture of a 'West Country' hauling a goods train. Eastleigh based No.34019 BIDEFORD was photographed near Beaulieu Road, with a Down train of empty clay wagons, in August 1965. The wagons were destined for Furzebrook, railhead for the clay traffic coming out of the Isle of Purbeck. At its' height, such traffic totalled 30,000 tons a year and even in 1981, three years before cessation of the traffic, 21,000 tons was carried. Entering traffic as Southern Railway No.21C119, on Christmas Eve 1945, the Bullied lasted in its original form until withdrawal on 19th March 1967, with 701,316 miles run. The Pacific was cut up at Cashmore's, Newport in September, the same year. British Railways shed allocations: Exmouth Junction; March 1951 Nine Elms; September 1958 Brighton; August 1963 Salisbury; August 1964 Feltham; November 1964 Eastleigh; June 1966 Nine Elms. *(BLP - S49)*

Watched by a Class H 0-4-4T, waiting in the bay platform with a Hawkhurst branch train, the highly effective, but oh, so unlovely, Class Q1 0-6-0 is represented here by No.33034 running through Paddock Wood station with a Dover bound freight, in June 1960. This Bulleid design of the wartime austerity years used no unnecessary materials in its construction, which gave a very basic, but very strong machine - just what was required in wartime. All forty locomotives came into British Railways ownership and gave sterling service in the Eastern and Central sections of the Southern Region until the last was withdrawn in January 1966. The doyen of the class was preserved as part of the National Collection, but normally resides on the Bluebell Railway. No.33034 was built in 1942 and withdrawn in January 1964, but was noted over five months later at 87D Swansea East Dock shed, doubtless on its way to a scrapyard. BR shed allocations: Tonbridge; May 1961 Guildford. *(BLP - S64)*

Class B4 0-4-0T No.30102 shunts the yard at Winchester L&SWR station, in August 1961. The B4 Dock Tanks were introduced by Adams in 1891 and were initially required to deal with the expansion of traffic in the many small yards of the L&SWR, particularly around the Plymouth area. Twenty engines were in service by 1892, with Drummond adding a further five, with detail differences, in 1907. They were destined for Southampton docks, where by the formation of the Southern Railway in 1923, fourteen were working. The same number was still present at the end of World War 2, but when faced with expensive overhauls, Bulleid purchased surplus USA tanks and the B4s started to go, some being scrapped but eleven sold on to industrial users. By 1963 only two were left, No.30096 and the engine pictured here. When they started working in Southampton docks, the B4s were given names, so today, No.96 NORMANDY, and 102 GRANVILLE, are preserved at the Bluebell Railway and the Bressingham steam museum, respectively. No.30102 was withdrawn in September 1963; British Railways shed allocations: Plymouth Friary; September 1958 Eastleigh; February 1959 Bournemouth; October 1961 Eastleigh. *(BLP - S31)*

Un-rebuilt 'West Country' No.34015 EXMOUTH, sits beside the coal stack at Exmouth Junction shed in May 1959. This particular engine is notable for one or two points of detail. First, in the original Southern Railway naming list 21C106 was to be called Exmouth, but in fact that number went to Bude, while Exmouth took Bude's first planned number of 21C115. Also, in 1957, No.34015 was the last by a very good measure, to receive the V-type cab applied to the un-rebuilt engines to help with the problem of drifting smoke. EXMOUTH remained un-rebuilt and survived into the last year of steam, being withdrawn on 16th April 1967, before proceeding to Cashmore's, Newport for scrapping, in the following September. British Railways shed allocations: Salisbury; March 1951 Exmouth Junction; August 1964 Salisbury. *(BLP - S133)*

(opposite) A rare combination at Basingstoke in June 1960! 'Schools' Class No.30908 WESTMINSTER, double-heads with an unidentified Class N 2-6-0 on an Up local to Waterloo. Quite why such a train should have the luxury of two engines was not recorded, but a reasonable assumption is that the N was working up to the Capital, perhaps as a balancing working. Ninth locomotive of the first batch of 'Schools', No.908 emerged from Eastleigh works in September 1930 and was withdrawn in September 1961. British Railways shed allocations: St. Leonards; May 1957 Stewarts Lane; May 1959 Basingstoke.
Founded in the 12th century by the monks of Westminster Abbey, the 'College' survived the Reformation and the years up to 1963 when the first girl entered the previously all-male establishment. Today Westminster School continues to provide senior education for more than 700 pupils, still mostly boys. *(BLP - S107)*

Hauling a very lengthy Down freight, Class S15 No.30835 is seen near Farnborough in September 1963. As remarked elsewhere, the S15 was conceived by Urie as a small wheeled, freight version of the 'King Arthur' 4-6-0, and proved their utility and ubiquity by outlasting the 'King Arthurs' in service by more than three years. Because of their relatively late withdrawals many S15s found their way to places like Woodhams yard at Barry and therefore proved to be popular with the preservation movement. So much so that seven examples survive today - two Urie engines and five Maunsell: not all are in working order though. No.30835 was built as part of the 1936 batch and was withdrawn in December 1964. British Railways shed allocations: Feltham; July 1951 Redhill; June 1963 Feltham. *(BLP - S128)*

(opposite) Class M7 0-4-4T No.30251 simmers in the sunshine of an Eastleigh 'Open Day' in June 1960. A Nine Elms engine at the time, No.30251 was conveniently ex-works at the time to lend its' presence to the Eastleigh event. It is interesting to recall that (30)672 of this class had the questionable distinction of being involved in one of Britain's most bizarre railway accidents when, in 1948, she fell down the rolling stock lift shaft of the Waterloo and City Railway. Recovery intact was impossible so the M7 had to be cut up in situ for removal. No.30251 happily had a more normal end, being withdrawn in July 1963; British Railways shed allocations: Bournemouth; April 1951 Barnstaple Junction; January 1963 Feltham; March 1963 Eastleigh. *(BLP - S136)*

11

Hard work for 'West Country' No.34096 TREVONE, as she climbs to the eastern portal of Honiton tunnel, with a westbound express, in May 1959. British Railways was nearly two years old when 34096 was built, in November 1949. The engine was rebuilt in April 1961. The locomotive's record card unusually shows 'Work done at Stewarts Lane Electric Depot' between 3rd and 5th November 1962, but then tantalisingly fails to say what that work was - we may only speculate! No.34096's long tenure at Exmouth Junction depot ensured that she was an early casualty of the Western Region takeover, with withdrawal in September 1964, only three years after an expensive rebuild. Prior to the engine's move to Exmouth Junction in December 1957, her only other BR shed allocation had been at 74B Ramsgate. (BLP - S123)

Simmering in the afternoon sun at her home shed of Tonbridge in May 1958, is Class L 4-4-0 No.31762. Built to a design initiated by Wainwright, but amended and completed by Maunsell, South Eastern & Chatham Railway No.762 emerged from the Manchester works of Beyer, Peacock & Co. in August 1914. One of a class of twenty-two locomotives, twelve were built by Beyer, Peacock and the remaining ten by A.Borsig, of Berlin, Germany - these latter engines were delivered in June and July, 1914, literally at the last moment, before the onset of World War One! It is worth recounting that these particular locomotives were shipped over in pieces to Dover, and had their boilers and frames erected at Ashford by Borsig's own employees. Also they were the only express passenger types ever built in Germany, for a British railway, the only other motive power coming from there being a handful of minor engines and latterly, some diesel railcars. The German-built Class L had Schmidt superheaters while those from Beyer, Peacock had the Robinson type, a difference that does not seem to have caused any trouble with spares etc. Renumbered 1762 by the Southern Railway and then 31762 by British Railways, the advance of electrification in Kent rendered such engines surplus and No.31762 was withdrawn in January 1960. BR shed allocations: Ashford; January 1951 Tonbridge; May 1959 Nine Elms.
(BLP - S12)

'700' class 0-6-0 No.30306 poses at Eastleigh shed in June 1960, already sixty-three years old and with a further twenty-two months to withdrawal in April 1962. Designed by Drummond, but built by Dubs and Company, the Class 700's cylinders, motion, firebox and boiler, were standard with Classes C8, K10 and M7. There were some initial problems with the Class 700, mainly jamming regulators and broken axles, but once these were overcome, the thirty members of the type settled down to a long and successful career, the last not being withdrawn until December 1962. No.30306's British Railways shed allocations were: Eastleigh; November 1956 Bournemouth; March 1957 Eastleigh. *(BLP - S137)*

(opposite) Near the end of its working life, Class D1 4-4-0 No.31735 is seen at its then home shed of Eastleigh, in June 1960. The D1 type came about through Maunsell's constant problem: deal with increasing train weights, but keep within light axle loadings. Following his very successful rebuilds of Wainwright's Class E to E1, Maunsell simply did the same to Wainwright's Class D. Starting in 1921 with ten locomotives being rebuilt by Beyer, Peacock (due to limited capacity at Ashford), a further eleven Ds were rebuilt to D1 by 1927 and brought about one of the best 4-4-0 types ever seen in Britain. All but one came into British Railways ownership with most surviving to the end of the 1950s and start of the 1960s. South Eastern & Chatham Railway No.735 was one of the batch rebuilt by Beyer, Peacock in 1921 and, as No.31735, was withdrawn in April 1961. BR shed allocations: Gillingham; March 1951 Tonbridge; March 1952 Ashford; June 1952 Tonbridge; October 1952 Bricklayers Arms; February 1953 Redhill; July 1953 Bricklayers Arms; May 1959 Nine Elms; July 1959 Eastleigh. (A somewhat itinerant locomotive!) *(BLP - S138)*

16

Seen opposite 'Battle of Britain' Pacific No.34057 BIGGIN HILL, sizzles quietly in a bay platform at Basingstoke, in September 1964. A little while later, (above) 34057 pulls out with its' Down local for the Bournemouth line. In the background one of the numerous British Railways Standard Class 4 2-6-0 allocated new to the Southern Region (76005-76019, 76025-76029, 76053-76069), waits for its next turn of duty. One of the six 'Battle of Britain' class engines named for a fighter station, No.34057 began service on 8th March 1947. It was never rebuilt and survived almost to the end, being withdrawn on 7th May 1967, having covered 939,957 miles. British Railways shed allocations: Nine Elms; March 1951 Exmouth Junction; April 1951 30A Stratford (Eastern Region, for trials purposes); May 1952 Exmouth Junction; October 1954 Salisbury; November 1954 Exmouth Junction; October 1960 Brighton; August 1963 Salisbury.

RAF Biggin Hill was home to the Biggin Hill Sector Operations Room and Staff, and the following Squadrons during the Battle: 32 Sqn, 72 Sqn (twice), 74 Sqn, 79 Sqn (twice), 92 Sqn, 141 Sqn, 610 Sqn. (BLP - S152 & S108)

The primary reason for the longevity of the ex-London Brighton & South Coast 'Terrier' 0-6-0T was the branch line from Havant to Hayling Island, with the lengthy, wooden Langstone bridge that could support only the lightest of locomotives. Here A1X No.32640 is seen at Langstone flats, near the north end of the bridge, in July 1962. No.32640 had an illustrious past. Completed in March 1878 as LBSCR Class A1 No.40 BRIGHTON, the engine was immediately exhibited at the Paris Exhibition where it won a gold medal. In 1902 No.40 was purchased by the Isle of Wight Central Railway, receiving their number 11. Rebuilding to A1X took place in August 1918 and eventually of course the engine came into the Southern Railway at Grouping, later receiving the name NEWPORT. The SR repatriated the locomotive to the mainland in 1947 as No.2640, soon to become British Railways No.32640. Withdrawal came in September 1963 but the engine was bought by the Isle of Wight Steam Railway and once again transported to the island, where it resides today. BR shed allocations: Brighton; March 1951 Newhaven (75A sub-shed); May 1952 Fratton; July 1952 St.Leonards; September 1952 Newhaven; May 1954 Fratton; October 1955 Brighton; May 1956 Fratton; November 1959 Eastleigh; June 1963 Brighton. The line from Havant was completed in two stages - first, the independent Hayling Island Railway opened from Havant to Langstone on 12th January 1865, (renamed Langston in May 1875), the temporary terminus being provided with an engine shed to house the locomotive of the contractor working the line. Completion of the bridge allowed extension to Hayling Island on 16th July 1867 with the contractor continuing to work all services until the LBSCR took over the line on lease, from January 1872. *(BLP - S26)*

(opposite) 'Terrier' No.32678 trundles its' two-coach Havant to Hayling Island train across the creaking Langstone bridge in April 1962. Built as London Brighton & South Coast Railway Class A1 No.78 KNOWLE, in June 1880, the engine was later renumbered to 678 and rebuilt to A1X in November 1911. Numbered 2678 by the Southern Railway, the engine was withdrawn in 1925 and stored for four years before being moved to the Isle of Wight, where it became W4 BEMBRIDGE. Returned to the mainland in 1936, the number 2678 was re-assumed, this becoming 32678 under British Railways, who finally withdrew the engine in October 1963. Then Mr Billy Butlin stepped in and on 25th July 1964, bought No.32678 for exhibition at Butlin's Minehead holiday camp, along with, of all things, ex LMS Pacific No.(4)6229 DUCHESS OF HAMILTON! There, in that seasonal corner of Somerset, KNOWLE languished until purchased by and moved to the Kent & East Sussex Railway, where she resides today. It was on the opening of the line to Hayling Island that a strange economy took place. The temporary engine shed at Langston was taken down, but instead of moving the materials for the few miles to Hayling, the former engine shed at Petworth, which had closed in 1866, was demolished and redeployed over a much greater distance, to become the locomotive depot for Hayling Island! That shed incidentally, was itself closed in 1894 leaving just a coal stage and water tank for the engines' use. A similar set of facilities existed at Havant, which meant that from 1894 until closure of the line on 4th November 1963, the 'Terriers' working the line (out-stationed from Fratton shed) stood all the time in the open. *(BLP - S96)*

A very pleasing portrait of a Bulleid Light Pacific at Exmouth Junction shed in May 1959. No.34034 HONITON still carries the old emblem on its tender, a sure sign that the engine is soon due to visit works. This she did, in mid-1960, emerging from a 'General' overhaul in rebuilt condition. Running until literally a week before the end of steam on the Southern, removal from traffic took place on 2nd July 1967. Total miles run by the engine were 942,133, of which 305,134 were as rebuild; British Railways shed allocations: Stewarts Lane; September 1950 Exmouth Junction; November 1950 Plymouth Friary; March 1952 Exmouth Junction; October 1961 Eastleigh; June 1966 Nine Elms. *(BLP - S95)*

Beattie's London & South Western Railway 0298 class 2-4-0 Well Tanks were known as the oldest working steam locomotives on British Railways, but just how much of the locomotives remained to deserve that accolade is debatable! Nevertheless, venerable they were, with a design dating back to 1862 and the last three not being withdrawn until the end of 1962. They owed their survival simply to the Bodmin & Wenford Railway's line to Wenford Bridge, which because of its curvature, necessitated engines with a very short wheelbase. The first Class 0298 arrived, by sea, in 1892 and three of the class were working on the line by 1895. They included 298, which as Southern Railway 3298 and then BR No.30587, carried on with those same duties until withdrawal, a total of more than sixty-seven years! The locomotive pictured here, No.30586, ex-works at Wadebridge shed in June 1960, was the only one of the trio with square splashers and sadly, the only one of them to be scrapped after being withdrawn. She was built by Beyer, Peacock & Co. in 1875 as L&SWR No.329, becoming SR No.3329. All her BR work was carried out from Wadebridge shed (72F). *(BLP - S7)*

Freshly cleaned for her trip to Wenford Bridge, 0298 class 2-4-0WT No.30585 shines in the sun at Wadebridge depot, in June 1960. Built in 1873 by Beyer, Peacock & Co. as L&SWR No.314, she ended up, in 1899, at Wadebridge, along with her two sisters, the only survivors of a class of eighty-five engines. They continued working the local lines until 1921 when all received new boilers, based on the Drummond 1907 pattern for the Class O2 0-4-4T. Then, in 1931, No.314 suffered a frame failure and received a new one of modified pattern; Nos.328 and 329 were subsequently similarly altered, leaving little of the original locomotives intact. Like her sisters, No.30585 ended her working days when some ex-Great Western Railway 0-6-0 Pannier tanks, of unique design, became redundant from working around the docks at Weymouth. Accordingly, Nos.1367 and 1369 were moved to Wadebridge in July 1962, where they saw out the days of steam, both being withdrawn in October 1964. Wadebridge shed had opened with the North Cornwall Railway's arrival in the town, 1st June 1895. Coded 72F by British Railways, the depot was re-coded to 84E (ex-Tyseley, Great Western) on 9th September 1963. The shed was formally closed in October 1964 but remained available for servicing visiting locomotives until the next year. Demolished in 1969, private housing now covers its site. *(BLP - S79)*

Rebuilt 'Battle of Britain' No.34085 501 SQUADRON, nears Hinton Admiral in July 1965, with a Bournemouth -Sheffield train, composed mostly of ex-London Midland and Scottish Railway stock. Opened on 6th March 1888 as Hinton, the station hereabouts was renamed Hinton Admiral for Highcliffe-on-Sea L&SW on 1st May 1888 and then at an unknown date, renamed again, to Hinton Admiral, by British Railways. One of the BR built Bullied's, No.34085 was completed on 19th November 1948 and was rebuilt in June 1960, after running 441,609 miles. In rebuilt form the engine ran for another 219,806 miles, up to withdrawal on 26th September 1965. BR shed allocations: Stewarts Lane; April 1951 Ramsgate; February 1958 Dover; March 1958 Stewarts Lane; January 1961 Eastleigh.

501 Squadron was formed at Filton Aerodrome, Bristol, in 1929 as a Special Reserve light bomber unit. Redesignated as a fighter squadron at the end of 1938 and equipping with Hurricanes, the unit fought first in France and then during the Battle of Britain, from Croydon and Gravesend. *(BLP - S50)*

'Lord Nelson' Class No.30854 HOWARD OF EFFINGHAM spent all its British Railways' service working from 71A Eastleigh shed, where it is seen in April 1960, standing in front of one of the depot's breakdown train tool vans. In its' original form the class featured a single chimney and attained a reputation for being not very good steamers, although this may have partly been due to the small number of engines in the class and therefore relative unfamiliarity with the men as to the best way of firing. However, when Bulleid succeeded Maunsell he fitted the 'Lord Nelsons' with Lemaitre multiple blast pipes and larger piston valves, both of which led to better all-round performance. Coming into service in October 1928, HOWARD OF EFFINGHAM was withdrawn in September 1961, to be cut up at Eastleigh works.

Charles Howard was a cousin of Queen Elizabeth I and in 1573, at the age of thirty-seven, he succeeded to his father's title of Lord Howard of Effingham. In 1585, despite having relatively little maritime experience, he was made Lord Admiral of England and in that capacity he led the English fleet against the Spanish Armada in 1588. Sensibly he deferred tactical control to his more experienced second in command, Sir Francis Drake and the consequent victory over the Spanish. Later taking part in the successful assault on Cadiz, for which he was created Earl of Nottingham, Howard saw many other high posts and their rewards before his death in 1624. *(BLP - S84)*

'Merchant Navy' Class No.35020 BIBBY LINE approaches Basingstoke with an Up express in September 1964, the month in which electrification of the Bournemouth services was announced, thus presaging the end of mainline steam in Southern England. The two Siphon Gs behind the locomotive suggest perhaps, a boat train from Southampton, with passengers' luggage being loaded in the Siphons. The locomotive entered traffic as 21C20 on 30th June 1945 and it was the fracture of this engine's driving axle, at speed near Crewkerne, on 24th April 1953, that caused the temporary withdrawal from traffic for tests, of the entire class. Rebuilt in March/April 1956, No.35020 was withdrawn in February 1965, having run 981,479 miles; she was the only member of her class to be scrapped at Eastleigh works. British Railways shed allocations: Nine Elms; August1964 Weymouth.

The Bibby Line itself was formed in 1805 by John Bibby of Liverpool and unlike many shipping companies of the past is still in business today, having diversified into the oil exploitation industry with rigs and barges, as well as maintaining a fleet of tankers. *(BLP - S9)*

A quintessential English scene as Mr Pirt captures Class H 0-4-4T No.31177 ambling along with its two ancient coaches through flower-bedecked fields, a reminder of an age when things moved much more - slowly. The location is near Brasted, on the branch line from Dunton Green to Westerham, with the train heading for Westerham; the date is June 1960. No.31177 continued for a short while longer on such duties until closure of lines like Dunton Green to Westerham, the engine being withdrawn in October 1961. BR shed allocations: Stewarts Lane; March 1951 Tonbridge. The 4⅝ mile branch line to Westerham was promoted by the Westerham Valley Railway Company and opened on 7th July 1881, being worked by the South Eastern Railway from the outset and being vested in that company later the same year. The line's placid path through time ended with total closure on 30th October 1961; few traces remain today. At first the branch engine was stabled in a small shed at Westerham which was closed by the Southern Railway in 1925, with the branch train thereafter travelling out each day from Tonbridge. However, water supplies remained available at the terminus and there was a locomotive servicing facility of some sort at Dunton Green. *(BLP - S174)*

Exmouth Junction engine shed in May 1959 comprised a twelve road concrete building with a northlight concrete roof, which had opened, in stages, during 1926-27. It replaced an eleven road LSWR shed that stood on a site just further west (roughly where Mr Pirt was standing), that had been built of corrugated iron in 1887 and could only be described as a total ruin by the time it closed! The LSWR's first shed in Exeter was actually a Yeovil & Exeter Railway three road building in stone, that stood at the south east end of Exeter Queen Street (later, Central) station, opening on 1st June 1861. Even after opening of the first depot at Exmouth Junction, Queen Street shed was not demolished until 1904 and then the coal stage and turntable remained in use until March 1931. Exmouth Junction was the site of one of the few mechanical coaling towers employed by the LSWR/SR/ BR (SR), others being at Nine Elms, Feltham, Stewarts Lane and Ramsgate. This was because the Welsh coal mainly used by the railways did not stand up too well to the rough handling it received in a mechanical coaler, a problem largely solved at the other four sites, where Yorkshire or Kentish coal was eventually introduced; Exmouth Junction used Welsh coal to the end. Coded 72A by BR, the depot came into Western Region purview on 9th September 1963 with a new code of 83D, recently relinquished by the ex-GWR shed at Laira, Plymouth. This marked the beginning of the end, with Exmouth Junction formally closing to steam in June 1965, followed by complete closure around April 1967. The building stood empty until demolition in 1970; a supermarket now covers the site. *(BLP - S180)*

Rebuilt 'West Country' No.34005 BARNSTAPLE nears Tonbridge with a Folkestone to London boat train, in June 1960. Completed in April 1945 the engine was named, at Barnstaple Town station, on 30th August 1946, by the town's mayor, Councillor R.Berry. Later, 34005 became the first Bulleid Light Pacific to be rebuilt after the fashion of the 'Merchant Navy' class, emerging from the works in the new guise in June 1957, after having run 498,808 miles. Withdrawal took place in October 1966, when another 347,524 miles had been covered, followed by scrapping at Buttgieg's yard, Newport. British Railways shed allocations: Exmouth Junction; March 1951 Nine Elms; May 1957 Stewarts Lane; December 1957 Bricklayers Arms; February 1961 Salisbury; October 1965 Bournemouth. *(BLP - S193)*

(opposite) Another K.R.Pirt classic, as Class 0298 No.30585 takes china clay empties onto the Wenford line at Boscarne Junction, on the line from Wadebridge to Bodmin, in June 1960. The Bodmin & Wadebridge Railway had opened its station in the town on 4th July 1834, this closing in November 1886. The London & South Western Railway opened a replacement station at Bodmin on 1st November 1895, this being renamed Bodmin (North) on 26th September 1949. Closure came on 31st January 1967. The line in the foreground of the picture is the ex-Great Western branch from its own station at Bodmin, opened 27th May 1887 and renamed Bodmin (General) on 26th September 1949. Like its ex-L&SWR counterpart, Bodmin (General) closed on 31st January 1967, but today is the headquarters of the Bodmin & Wenford Railway, which links Bodmin Parkway main line station, with Bodmin General and on to the site of the former Boscarne Junction, a total of six and a half miles. *(BLP - S162)*

35014 NEDERLAND LINE roars through Basingstoke with a Down express in September 1964. As 21C14, the locomotive entered traffic on 13th February 1945 and was named nine months later by Mr A.F.Bronsing, Managing Director of the shipping company. Rebuilt in July 1956, No.35014 ran 1,062,394 miles before being withdrawn in March 1967; cutting up occurred at Cashmore's yard, Newport six months later. BR shed allocations: Nine Elms; May 1954 Exmouth Junction; August 1954 Bournemouth; May 1955 Stewarts Lane; May 1956 Nine Elms; August 1964 Weymouth. In the picture's background can be seen Basingstoke engine shed, with an illustrious visitor, none other than preserved LNER Pacific No.4472 FLYING SCOTSMAN, which was being serviced between working the *FARNBOROUGH FLYER* special train for visitors to the then, annual Farnborough Airshow. The three road engine shed opened sometime in 1905, replacing a single road shed to the south east of the station, which itself had opened in 1858. Coded 70D by British Railways, the shed closed in March 1963, but was retained as a servicing and stabling point until the end of steam in July 1967; demolition took place two years later. The Nederland Line was formed in 1870 for the Holland-Dutch East Indies traffic, which continued until Indonesian independence in 1957. In 1960 Nederland Line merged with Rotterdam Lloyd to form Nedlloyd, which company still trades today. *(BLP - S40)*

Four-cylinder 'Lord Nelson' Class 4-6-0 No.30860 LORD HAWKE basks in the sunshine at Eastleigh shed in April 1960, still carrying the old 'Lion and Wheel' emblem. These locomotives were introduced as an answer to the need projected in 1925 for hauling 500 ton trains at an average speed of 55 m.p.h. Maunsell went a long way to keeping down the engine's weight to give it route availability and spent two years experimenting with the prototype before further machines were built. In fact the expected train weight/ average speed projections were never realised, but the LN class as they became designated, did prove capable of such performance, albeit in ideal conditions and then mostly, east of Salisbury. So, only a further fifteen engines were built, with the class having the distinction, at the time, of being the most powerful express passenger engines in Britain, in terms of tractive effort - something of a red herring, but manna from heaven for the publicity department! The engines were also unique in having their cranks set at 135 degrees with the drive divided between two axles, resulting in eight exhaust beats to the revolution instead of the normal four. In fact this feature applied to fifteen of the class - the last, No.865 SIR JOHN HAWKINS, had normal crank settings and gave out four beats per revolution. The sound put out by of the rest of the 'Nelsons' being worked can best be described perhaps, as a 'putter'. No.860 emerged from Eastleigh works in December 1929 and was withdrawn from service in August 1962, after covering well over a million miles. BR shed allocations: Nine Elms; May 1958 Bournemouth; November 1959 Eastleigh.

Admiral Sir Edward Hawke was the victor over the French fleet under the command of Admiral Conflans. Hawke had successfully blockaded the French in Brest harbour for many months, thereby forestalling an invasion of Britain, but in November 1759 Hawke had to retire out to sea because of bad weather, allowing the French fleet to escape. Undaunted he gave chase, leading the British fleet from his flagship HMS Royal George and finally brought the French to action and a decisive defeat, at the Battle of Quiberon Bay. Hawke returned in triumph to Britain, where a grateful nation elevated him to the title of Lord Hawke.; he died in 1781. *(BLP - S3)*

'Battle of Britain' No.34067 TANGMERE, lays down a smoke screen as she races towards Paddock Wood with a boat express for Folkestone in June 1960. As 21C167, the locomotive was out-shopped on 3rd September 1947, being named sixteen days later, at Brighton, by Wing Commander Clouston RAF. No.34067 was not rebuilt and reached the end of her British Railways service life on 16th November 1963. British Railways shed allocations: Stewarts Lane; May 1961 Salisbury; October 1963 'to Western Region'. (Whether this inter-regional transfer did take place is conjectural, but most likely, because of the almost immediate and early withdrawal!). Despite a relatively early demise, a stay at Woodham's Barry, ensured 34067 was saved for preservation and today is owned by the Mid-Hants Railway. However, being passed for mainline running, and a favourite for hauling the Venice Simplon Orient Express luxury train, 34067 currently spends most of its time working from Network Rail depots.

RAF Tangmere was home to the Tangmere Sector Operations Room and Staff, and the following Squadrons during the Battle of Britain: 17 Sqn, 43 Sqn, 145 Sqn (twice); 213 Sqn, 266 Sqn, 601 Sqn (twice); 607 sqn. *(BLP - S194)*

(opposite) A Stroudley Class A1X 0-6-0T, No.32636 waits at what purports to be a wayside station on the Kent & East Sussex Railway, in April 1958. The Class A1 was introduced in 1872 and despite the diminutive size the design - later nicknamed the 'Terrier' - can be considered to have been very successful as the last survivors were not withdrawn until 1963! No.32636 itself was delivered as London Brighton & South Coast Railway No.72, carrying the name FENCHURCH; in fact she was the first A1 to enter service. No.72 was sold to the Newhaven Harbour Company in 1898, was rebuilt to A1X in April 1913 and re-purchased in 1927 by the Southern Railway, which allocated the number 2636 to the locomotive. Passing into British Railways' stock as No.32636, the Terrier was finally withdrawn in November 1963, soon afterwards being purchased by the Bluebell Railway, where she continues to reside today. BR shed allocations: Brighton; August 1953 Newhaven (75A sub-shed); October 1955 St.Leonards; May 1958 Ashford; October 1959 Fratton; November 1959 Eastleigh; February 1960 Brighton. The Kent & East Sussex Light Railway opened, as the Rother Valley (Light) Railway, for goods traffic on 29th March 1900; passenger services started four days later. Various extensions completed the line throughout from Robertsbridge to Headcorn on 15th May 1905, with the company name having been changed to the K&ESLR the previous year. Never really paying its way, the line staggered on to come into BR ownership but, despite an increase of services, traffic never followed suit, so the section from Tenterden to Headcorn closed to all traffic on 4th January 1954, leaving the Robertsbridge-Tenterden section to continue supporting good traffic until final closure 12th June 1961. Since that time preservationists have reopened part of the line and created a very successful tourist attraction. Locomotives working the line pre-preservation were kept in a two-road shed at Rolvenden which formally closed on 2nd January 1954. *(BLP - S2)*

With drain cocks hissing and safety valve blowing, 'WC' 34023 BLACKMORE VALE moves off Basingstoke shed prior to hauling a local train to Waterloo, in September 1964. The engine record card shows that 21C123 entered traffic on 4th February 1946 and then over the next five months, spent three periods of three days at Ashford works, for "Non-classified" attention. After that things settled down and No.34023 went through to the last day of steam, being retired on 9th July 1967, with 'WC' No.34102 LAPFORD, the last two un-rebuilt Bulleid Pacifics in service. Unlike No.34102 though, BLACKMORE VALE was preserved and today resides on the Bluebell Railway. British Railways shed allocations: Salisbury; April 1951 Exmouth Junction; October 1963 Bournemouth; August 1964 Eastleigh; April 1967 Nine Elms. *(BLP - S124)*

(opposite) No.30857 LORD HOWE, rests between duties in the yard at Eastleigh shed, accompanied at the rear by an ex-works USA class 0-6-0 tank. It is an interesting fact that the 'Lord Nelson' class had a fire grate which was unique among Southern locomotives, in that it was horizontal at the rear while the front was steeply inclined. This provided an area of 33 sq. ft., which at the time of introduction was the largest of any British locomotive. No.857 left Eastleigh works in November 1928 and spent most of its working life at Eastleigh depot - certainly all its' time under BR was spent working from there. The engine was withdrawn in September 1962, along with sister locomotive No.30856 LORD ST.VINCENT and in the next month the class was rendered extinct with the withdrawal of the last two 'Lord Nelsons'; happily, the class doyen is preserved and hopefully will be running on the main line again in the not too distant future.

Admiral Lord Howe had commanded the English Fleet during the American War of Independence and had been stopped by the French navy from rescuing the English army at Yorktown. Suitable revenge was taken, however, when Lord Howe, in command of twenty-five ships, met a French fleet of twenty-six ships in what became known as the battle of the Glorious First of June (1794), when a sharp defeat was suffered by the French in the first sea battle of the French Revolutionary War. For his success Lord Howe was created a Knight of the Garter (not until 1983 was the second, naval Knight of the Garter created; Admiral of the Fleet Lord Lewin), and he died in 1799. *(BLP - S192)*

Tonbridge station in June 1960, with 'Schools' No.30936 CRANLEIGH, awaiting departure with a train for London. This single-chimney locomotive was part of the last batch of ten of the Maunsell-designed, 3-cylinder engines to be outshopped from Eastleigh, in July 1935. With the exception of the last fourteen months up to its withdrawal in December 1962, it is believed this engine spent all her working life on the former Southern Railway's Eastern Section. British Railways shed allocations: Bricklayers Arms; May 1959 Ashford; October 1961 Nine Elms.
Cranleigh School was founded in 1865 as a boys' boarding school, sixth form girls began to arrive in the early 1970s. Cranleigh now has over 600 pupils and is fully co-educational. *(BLP - S78)*

(opposite) Wainwright Class H 0-4-4T No.31519 waits to leave Hawkhurst with a branch train to Paddock Wood, in June 1960, one year before the line was closed to passenger traffic. The Class H was introduced by the South Eastern & Chatham Railway for handling the increasingly heavy suburban traffic, with sixty-six of the engines being constructed at Ashford works, between 1904 and 1915. Though the SE&CR was largely a vacuum-braked railway, sixteen locomotives were fitted with Westinghouse brakes for working air-braked stock; some were later fitted for push-pull working. Their resulting general usefulness ensured that sixty-four engines survived to come into British Railways use; two had been withdrawn during World War 2 with cracked frames. The remains of the two casualties were not scrapped however, being retained as a source of spares. A few withdrawals occurred in the early 1950s, with large scale removal from service starting in 1959, occasioned by the Kent Coast Electrification; the last survivor, No.31263 went in January 1964. This locomotive pictured here was withdrawn in March 1961. BR shed allocations: Ramsgate; May 1952 St.Leonards; February 1953 Tonbridge; March 1953 Faversham; May 1958 Ashford; June 1959 Tonbridge. The branch line from Paddock Wood to Hawkhurst was opened on 4th September 1893, by the privately promoted Cranbrook & Paddock Wood Company, being worked by the South Eastern Railway from the outset. As mentioned above, the branch closed in 1961 but today, the two-road engine shed and goods shed at Hawkhurst still stand, albeit in private use. *(BLP - S8)*

Rebuilt 'West Country' No.34048 CREDITON rushed through Basingstoke with a Down Bournemouth express in April 1960: what appears to be a Urie 4-6-0 and a BR Standard 4-6-0 are spectators at Basingstoke shed. Situated seven miles north west of Exeter, Crediton is an important market town, significant as being the birthplace, in 680AD, of Winfrith, later the martyred St. Boniface, Patron Saint of both Holland and Germany. The locomotive CREDITON was completed on 30th November 1946, being rebuilt in March 1959, and then running 307,627 miles until withdrawal on 13th March 1966. Total miles run by 34048 were 847,615; British Railways shed allocations: Salisbury; June 1951 Brighton; February 1959 Bournemouth; February 1960 Salisbury. *(BLP - S82)*

(opposite) Former United States Army Transportation Corps 0-6-0T No.30066 is seen in black, ex-works livery at Eastleigh shed in April 1960. Fifteen of these basic, but powerful locomotives were purchased by the Southern Railway specifically to replace life-expired Class B4 0-4-0T working in Southampton docks. The Southern's 'USA's' as they were known, came from two American builders - thirteen from Vulcan Ironworks and two from Porter. Even then only one of the Porter-built engines was taken into stock; the other was dismantled for spares. Highly successful in their role of dock tanks, the 0-6-0Ts were replaced by diesel shunting locomotives in 1962, whereupon six of the USAs were transferred to Departmental duties, including No.30066. This Porter-built, locomotive of 1942, formerly carried USATC number 1279, being taken into Southern stock in May 1947. In March 1963, No.30066 became DS235, employed at Lancing carriage works, and was finally withdrawn in August 1965. British Railways shed allocation: Southampton Docks. *(BLP - S65)*

In 1895 Dugald Drummond became Locomotive Superintendent of the London & South Western Railway and his first design, the Class M7 0-4-4T, appeared two years later, derived from his North British Railways Class 157, of 1877. Further batches of M7 followed until 1911, when the hundred and fifth, and last, was delivered. Numerous detail differences occurred within the class - too many to mention here. Suffice it to say that the M7 was a very successful design and all but two of the class entered British Railways ownership. All had been withdrawn by May 1964 with two members being preserved: No.30245 at the National Railway Museum and No.30053 at the Swanage Railway, via a sojourn in the USA. Pictured here is No.30480, ex-works at Eastleigh shed, in June 1960; she was withdrawn in May 1964. BR shed allocations: Fratton; March 1951 Eastleigh; January 1963 Bournemouth. *(BLP - S105)*

Pugnacious and business-like would describe Maunsell's Class Z 0-8-0T heavy shunting engine, here represented by No.30951, at Ashford shed, in May 1958. The class of eight engines was built to a requirement for a locomotive capable of delivering great power, even after lengthy periods of idling, and to do so without excessive blowing off and slipping. Quietness of operation and the ability to negotiate tight curves were also paramount. To achieve this a large steaming capacity was specified, using a parallel, non-superheated boiler with a grate area of 18.6 sq. ft and total evaporative heating surface of 1279 sq. ft. Boiler pressure of 180 lb per sq. in, three, 16 x 28 inch cylinders and 4ft 8in wheels, resulted in a tractive effort at 85 percent pressure of 29,380 lb. Despite the 17 ft 6 in wheelbase, curves of 4° chains could be negotiated. Both vacuum and steam brakes were fitted as was a steam reverser and steam heating for passenger stock and banana vans. The overall result was a powerful, flexible engine with a quiet beat, which was practically immune to slipping. Built by Brighton Works in 1929, No.30951 was withdrawn, along with all her sisters, in November 1962. The British Railways shed allocations: Gillingham; February 1953 Three Bridges; October 1955 Ashford; May 1959 Exmouth Junction. *(BLP - S125)*

Putting BR Standard Class 5 No.73082 CAMELOT firmly in its place, 'Merchant Navy' No.35008 ORIENT LINE on a Down express, overtakes the 4-6-0 with a Down local, near Farnborough in September 1963. The Pacific came into traffic on 16th June 1942 and was named five months later by Mr L.Geddes, Chairman of the Orient Line. 21C8 was out-shopped in black livery and bore that until repainted in green in August 1947, a visit to the works being occasioned by the Pacific colliding with an electric train at Waterloo, on 10th June 1947. ORIENT LINE was rebuilt in May 1957, having run nearly three quarters of a million miles and unusually, had a light casual repair in the workshop at Bricklayers Arms during June 1961. A general overhaul later that year was her last but 35008 went through to the end of steam in July 1967, afterwards being stored at Nine Elms shed for eight months before being hauled to Buttigiegs, Newport for scrapping - total mileage run was 1,286,418. BR shed allocations: Salisbury; January 1954 Bournemouth; August 1954 Exmouth Junction; February 1960 Bournemouth; October 1966 Weymouth; March 1967 Nine Elms. Standard Class 5 No.73082 entered service at Stewarts Lane shed in June 1955, moving to Nine Elms in May 1959. During 1960 the 4-6-0 received the name CAMELOT, formerly carried by 'King Arthur' Class 4-6-0 No.30782 which had been withdrawn from service at the end of 1956. No.73082 was reallocated to Guildford in May 1965 and was withdrawn in July 1966, to be moved to Woodhams, Barry. Saved in 1979 by the Camelot Locomotive Society; 73082 today works on the Bluebell Railway.

The Orient Steam Navigation Company was formed in 1877 chartering steamers to Australia. The name changed to Orient-Royal Mail in 1906 and the company was acquired by the Peninsular & Orient Line in 1919, with the name Orient Line finally being dropped in 1966. *(BLP - S103)*

Class T9 4-4-0 No.30313 waits at Wadebridge with an Up train to Exeter in June 1960. Note that the locomotive is fitted with a small six-wheeled tender and is one of the T9s built with wide splashers over both driving wheels and rods. Built at Nine Elms in May 1901, No.30313 was fitted with superheating in July 1922 and was withdrawn in July 1961. BR shed allocations: Eastleigh; April 1951 Guildford; June 1954 Salisbury; August 1959 Exmouth Junction. The line through Wadebridge to Padstow was opened on 27th March 1899 by the North Cornwall Railway, a London & South Western Railway subsidiary; thus was completed what became known by some as 'The Withered Arm'. Such derogation was not fully justified because the line traversed an area of great beauty and in its early days at least, yielded much goods traffic. But, passenger carryings were sparse except for three or four summer months and it really was not a surprise when British Railways had to close all the former LSWR lines west of Okehampton as an economic measure; the end actually came on 30th January 1967. *(BLP - S144)*

Maunsell Class S15 4-6-0 No.30842 undertakes some last minute shunting in Basingstoke Down yard before working a fitted freight to Salisbury, in September 1963. Originally designed by Urie as a smaller-wheeled version of his N15 'King Arthur' class 4-6-0, for fast, heavy freight work, the S15 was continued by Maunsell, with detail alterations, until forty-five engines were in service. Incidentally, the last built, in 1936, No.847, was also the last 4-6-0 built by the Southern Railway. No.30842 was part of that last batch of ten engines to appear in that year, working in freight and summer passenger service, until being withdrawn in September 1965. British Railways shed allocations: Exmouth Junction; August 1963 Feltham; December 1964 Basingstoke; January 1965 Feltham; June 1965 Basingstoke. *(BLP - S19)*

The fireman is working hard as 'Battle of Britain' No.34086 219 SQUADRON races south near Paddock Wood, with the prestigious *GOLDEN ARROW* Pullman express, in June 1960. This famous train was inaugurated jointly by the Southern Railway and Nord Railway of France, on 15th April 1929, and ran, except during the wartime emergency, until 1972. No.34086 entered service on 2nd December 1948, wearing an experimental apple green livery, which was replaced in October 1950 with the standard British Railways livery. Remaining un-rebuilt, 219 SQUADRON was withdrawn on 25th June 1966 having run 700,982 miles. BR shed allocations: Ramsgate; September 1957 Exmouth Junction; February 1958 Dover; March 1958 Stewarts Lane; May 1961 Exmouth Junction; August 1964 Eastleigh.

No.219 (Night Fighter) Squadron was formed at Catterick in 1939 and flew Blenheim night fighters from there and Leeming during the night raids of the Battle of Britain. The squadron re-equipped with Beaufighters in October 1940. *(BLP - S17)*

Ex-London & South Western Railway Class O2 0-4-4T, W27 MERSTONE, stands in the yard at Ryde, Isle of Wight, engine shed, in April 1962. An Adams design of 1888, the Class O2 numbered sixty engines by 1893, with the final ten having slightly higher roofs than their earlier sisters. A very successful design, the O2 proved ideal for the Southern Railway's standardisation of the hotchpotch locomotive stock inherited from the Isle of Wight railway companies, with the first nine 0-4-4T being moved there around 1925 to be joined by a further fourteen engines - the last two, not until 1949. As 'Islanders' the O2 were named, fitted with the Westinghouse brake and, from 1932, an enlarged coal bunker. The class remained staple power for the Island services until, with the exception of the Ryde-Shanklin section, all remaining lines were closed, on 31st December 1966, the steam locomotives going with them. MERSTONE was formerly Southern Railway No.184 and was withdrawn on the final day of steam working. British Railways shed allocations: Newport I.o.W; October 1957 Ryde I.o.W. *(BLP - S15)*

Leaving Ryde with a train for Ventnor is Class O2 W24 CALBOURNE, in April 1962. Originally built at Nine Elms in 1891, Southern Railway No.209 was moved to the Isle of Wight on 26th April 1925 and remained there until the finish of steam at the end of 1966. W24 was not officially withdrawn until March 1967, being bought for preservation. Today the locomotive is part of the stock of the Isle of Wight Steam Railway, but currently not in working order. British Railways shed allocation: Ryde I.o.W. The line from Ryde to Ventnor was opened in stages: Ryde, St. Johns Road to Shanklin on 23rd August 1864, with a temporary engine shed being provided at Shanklin while it was a railhead. On 10th September 1866, the three-quarters of a mile tunnel under St. Boniface down was completed and trains started running through Wroxall, to Ventnor. That extension lasted just under one hundred years as the route beyond Shanklin was closed by British Railways on 18th April 1966. *(BLP - S27)*

Although the Southern Railway imported twenty-three Class O2 0-4-4T's into the Isle of Wight, a handful of Class A1X 'Terriers' also worked there until the last returned to the mainland in 1949. In addition, four ex-London Brighton & South Coast Class E1 0-6-0T served on the Island, these basically being a goods version of the 'Terrier'. Numbered W1 to W4, the E1's were based at Newport I.o.W shed, with W1 and W2 being withdrawn in March 1957 and October 1956, respectively. W3 and W4 survived long enough to be moved to Ryde shed in October 1957 and W4 WROXHALL, is seen there, in unlined black goods livery, in April 1958. Built at Brighton in October 1878, as LB&SCR No.131 and named GOURNAY, she became Southern Railway B131 before being moved to the Isle of Wight in June 1933. W4 WROXHALL was finally withdrawn in October 1960, the last of her class on the island. That is not the complete story of the Southern Railway's attempts at finding locomotives for the Isle of Wight. In 1947 Billinton Class E4 0-6-2T No.2510 was based at Newport I.o.W and trialled on the Island's railways, but despite some success no more of the type was taken there and No.2510 returned to the mainland in 1949. Built by the LB&SCR at Brighton, in December 1900, No.510 became Southern Railway 2510, then after its' sojourn in the Isle of Wight, British Railways No.32510, working from 71A Eastleigh shed until withdrawal in October 1962. *(BLP - S58)*

Class O2 0-4-4T W26 WHITWELL, approaches Smallbrook Junction with a train for the line to Newport I.o.W, in April 1962. As No.210 of the Southern Railway, this O2 was moved to the Isle of Wight in 1925, going to Newport where she spent the next thirty-two years, before closure of that depot in October 1957 caused her to be moved to Ryde (70H). W26 was withdrawn in May 1966. The line from Smallbrook Junction to Newport was sponsored in 1872 by the Ryde & Newport Railway Company; it opened on 20th December 1875, with trains running into the Cowes & Newport Railway station at Newport, that had opened 16th June 1862. During construction of the Smallbrook Junction to Newport line, a temporary engine shed was situated at Ashey, this closing after the line was opened. British Railways closed the route on 21st February 1966, but since then the Isle of Wight Steam Railway has re-opened the five miles between Smallbrook Junction and Wootton, with a stud of locomotives that includes no less than three former Isle of Wight residents, Class A1X 'Terriers' W8 FRESHWATER and W11 NEWPORT and Class O2 W24 CALBOURNE. *(BLP - S29)*

W32 BONCHURCH sparkles in ex-works condition at Ryde, Isle of Wight shed, in April 1958. This Class O2 was numbered 226 by the Southern Railway before being moved to the island, where she worked out her days until withdrawal in October 1964. British Railways shed allocations: Newport I.o.W; October 1957 Ryde. The engine shed at Ryde hosting BONCHURCH was, in fact, the third in the town. The first, a two-road brick structure of 1864, was closed ten years later and incorporated into Ryde St. Johns works and as such, it exists today. The second shed was a two-road wooden building with a 'Dutch Barn' roof that by 1930, was in a parlous state. Accordingly the Southern replaced it with one of their ubiquitous concrete structures, again of two roads, that closed with the end of steam, on 31st December 1966. The Isle of Wight supported nine other engine sheds: One-road temporary structures at Shanklin (1864-1866) and Ashey (1873-1875), a two-road wooden shed at Newport (1875-1957), single road wooden sheds at Cowes (1862-1896), Newport (Freshwater, Yarmouth & Newport Railway) (1913-1923) and St. Helens, Bembridge (1882-1921) and three separate one-road sheds at Freshwater (1888-1890; 1890-1923 and 1908-1923). There was also an engine servicing line with a pit and water tank, at Sandown, opened in 1875 and closed at a date yet to be determined. (BLP - S127)

'Schools' Class No.30904 LANCING rests at Basingstoke - her home shed - in April 1960, before working to London with a local train. This highly successful class of engines - the most powerful 4-4-0 type to be built in Britain, first appeared in 1930, with ten engines coming from Eastleigh works between March and September of that year. Named after Public boarding schools, they saw service on the Southern Railway's Eastern section and later, most successfully, on the routes from Waterloo to Portsmouth and Bournemouth. No.30904 was built as SR 904 in July 1930 and was withdrawn precisely thirty one years later. British Railways shed allocations: St. Leonards; May 1957 Nine Elms; May 1958 Basingstoke.

Lancing School - or College as it is correctly known - was founded in 1848 by one Nathanial Woodard, Curate of New Shoreham. Today, the Anglican college still exists offering co-educational education to some 470 pupils aged between 13 and 18. Lancing was also the site chosen by the London Brighton & South Coast Railway, for an extensive carriage and wagon works, which opened in 1912. *(BLP - S14)*

The prestigious *BOURNEMOUTH BELLE* Pullman train nears Worting Junction in September 1964 with 35022 HOLLAND-AMERICA LINE at its head. The luxurious train was introduced by the Southern Railway in 1931 to cater for the increasing popularity of Bournemouth with the more well-off of Britain's travelling public. With only a few exceptions the train remained steam-hauled until the end of that form of traction in July 1967, from which point the all-Pullman train ran no more. Built under British Railways' auspices, No.35022 entered service on 9th October 1948 and was named at Southampton docks on 24th January 1949, by Mr W.H. de Monchy, the shipping line's Managing Director. The engine did not lose its Southern Railway style livery until 1952 - the last of her class to carry it. During 1952-54 the Pacific underwent various blastpipe trials at Rugby Testing Station and was rebuilt in June 1956 after having run just over 329,000 miles. In its rebuilt condition the locomotive ran a further 574,000 miles until withdrawn in May 1966 (actual mileage: 903,542), followed by five months storage before being moved to Dai Woodham's yard at Barry. No.35022 languished there until March 1986 when she was saved for preservation, at first moving to the Swanage Railway where further storage was succeeded by a move to a private location at Sellindge, Kent. There, the aim now is to restore the engine to its original condition - i.e. with Bulleid valve gear and air-smoothed casing. This seems an overly ambitious idea, but given what has gone before with other 'hopeless cases' (e.g. 71000 DUKE OF GLOUCESTER), who knows? BR allocations: Exmouth Junction; June 1952 Rugby Testing Plant; June 1954 Bournemouth; February 1960 Exmouth Junction; February 1964 Nine Elms; August 1964 Weymouth.

Formed in 1873 to exploit the burgeoning Europe-North America passenger and trade routes, the Holland-America Line is still in business today, largely concentrating on the world-wide cruise market. *(BLP - S42)*

Class 0415 4-4-2T No.30582 waits at Combpyne station with a train for Lyme Regis, in May 1959. The Class 415 (later 0415) were an Adams development of his earlier Class 46 4-4-0T, and were introduced to cater for increasing London suburban traffic, which they did, very successfully. Because Nine Elms works was at capacity, the final total of seventy-one engines were all built by outside contractors, while the Class 46 were all rebuilt as Atlantics, like the 415s. Thirty Class 0415 came into Southern Railway ownership, but by 1930, increasing electrification had reduced that to just two, Nos.0125 and 0520. These received a long-term reprieve when they were found to be ideal for working the sharply curved Axminster to Lyme Regis branch, so they were overhauled and re-entered service as Nos.3125 and 3520, to work the branch line well into British Railways days. By then they carried the numbers 30582 (ex-3125) and 30584 (ex-3520). All their time from 1930, therefore, was spent at Exmouth Junction depot (British Railways 72A), out-stationed at the small sub-shed at Lyme Regis. No.30582 was withdrawn in July 1961, with sister 30584 having gone six months earlier. (BLP - S6)

A fine portrait of Class 0415 4-4-2T No.30583, in the bay platform loop at Axminster station, in May 1959. Locomotive number 30583 had indeed, a very mixed history! Built by Neilson in 1883, as London & South Western Railway No.488, the engine was sold in 1917 to the Ministry of Munitions, only to be sold again, about 1920, to the renowned Colonel Stephens, of Light Railway fame. Col. Stephens employed the engine on the East Kent Railway, working from the engine shed at Shepherds Well, but by 1946 it was laid aside derelict, but intact. The Southern Railway had been searching for an additional locomotive for the Axminster to Lyme Regis branch so the 4-4-2T was purchased, overhauled, given the number 0488 and re-entered service working from Exmouth Junction depot, sub-shedded as required, at Lyme Regis. Coming into British Railways ownership, 0488 was re-numbered 30583 and was withdrawn in July 1961. But, unlike her two sisters, she survived again and was bought by the Bluebell Railway. Later overhauled in, of all places, Swindon works, L&SWR 488 worked on the Bluebell until 1990, by which time her boiler - an original, unlike those fitted to 30582 and 30584 - needed heavy repair or replacement, something that today, has still to be put in hand. *(BLP - S16)*

Resplendent in ex-works condition, Class 0415 30583 runs into Lyme Regis station with a late afternoon train from Axminster, in May 1959. Over the top of the coaches can be seen the roof of Lyme Regis engine shed, a corrugated asbestos structure which had been put up in 1913, to replace the original Axminster & Lyme Regis Light Railway depot - a wooden building that had the misfortune to burn down on 28th December 1912. A return trip with this locomotive and two coaches totalling 60 tons tare, 63 tons gross, was made on Sunday 24th July 1955. The 1.00 p.m. from Axminster made the journey to Lyme Regis in 20 minutes, 22 seconds, against a schedule of 21 minutes; maximum speed was 38 m.p.h. The 2.50 p.m. return took only 16 minutes, 21 seconds for the 21 minute timing, with a 33 m.p.h. maximum. Both trips included a stop at Combpyne. The Class 0415 engines saw service much beyond their years, only because their radial truck chassis enabled them to cope with the Lyme Regis branch's tight curvature. Eventually, however, in 1961, the 4-4-2Ts were replaced by Ivatt Class 2 2-6-2T, but only after track works to adapt the line to their use. *(BLP - S139)*

On summer Saturdays in British Railways times at least, loadings between Lyme Regis and Axminster were usually so heavy as to require double-heading by two of the three Class 0415 Atlantic tanks that worked the line until 1961. Here 30583 and 30582 with just such a heavy train wait to leave Combpyne (149 miles from London) for Axminster in May 1959. The April 1910 issue of *Bradshaw's Railway Guide*, shows weekdays only departures from Lyme Regis at 7.12 a.m., 9.38 a.m. (Fridays only), 9.48 a.m. (except Fridays), 12.30 p.m., 2.20 p.m., 3.55 p.m., 4.55 p.m., 6.30 p.m. and 8.15 p.m. From Axminster, times were, weekdays only: 8.5 a.m., 10.37 a.m., 1.7 p.m., 3.0 p.m., 4.27 p.m., 5.50 p.m., 7.12 p.m. and 8.45 p.m. From opening in 1903, Combpyne had a passing loop, but even with such a service as above, the average levels of traffic over the line did not justify such a luxury. Accordingly, the loop was removed in 1930. In later years though, some BR camping coaches were sited at this peaceful backwater (population circa 81 and some 1° miles from the station), surrounded as it is, by beautiful rolling countryside. *(BLP - S165)*

The Axminster to Lyme Regis branch packed a lot of features into its 6⅔ mile length! 1 in 40 gradients, numerous sharp curves and an impressive concrete viaduct at Cannington, which 4-4-2T 30582 has just crossed with a train from Axminster, in May 1959. The Axminster & Lyme Regis Railway was opened on 24th August 1903, being worked by the London & South Western Railway from the outset and absorbed by that company in 1907. Apart from 'normal' holidaymakers, the branch also saw much traffic in the early years from sightseers viewing a cliff landslip which occurred in 1839 and for some months in 1908, for those wanting to see a cliff fire between Charmouth and Lyme Regis. Gradually, however, road transport took away the passengers and although Ivatt Class 2 2-6-2T were drafted in to replace the venerable Class 0415 tanks, and then even diesel railcars were tried, the line closed to goods on 3rd February 1964 and totally, on 29th November 1965. *(BLP - S166)*

An ex-South Eastern & Chatham Railway Class C 0-6-0, No.31579, takes on fuel from the coal stage at Tonbridge shed in June 1960. A Wainwright design, the C class owed much to London Chatham & Dover Railway practice, in that they were simply, but robustly built, with a good turn of speed and riding qualities. Reliable in traffic they could frequently be seen on passenger work as well as the freight trains for which they were originally conceived. The first engines appeared in 1900 and in the succeeding eight years a further 107 were built. It is a tribute to their success that all but two of them came into British Railways ownership, with one (SE&CR 592) surviving today on the Bluebell Railway, after a spell in Departmental Stock. No.31579 was built at Ashford in October 1903 and was withdrawn exactly fifty-eight years later; BR shed allocations: Gillingham; April 1951 Stewarts Lane; September 1957 Gillingham; May 1959 Nine Elms; February 1960 Hither Green; June 1960 Feltham; December 1960 Stewarts Lane. The engine is recorded as being scrapped at Swinton, South Yorkshire. *(BLP - S198)*

Class N15 30764 SIR GAWAIN, gets away from a Brockenhurst stop with an Up express in April 1958. Note the superb telegraph pole with no fewer than twelve cross arms, each supporting four spans of copper wire. Such features were once common the length and breadth of Britain's railways, but nowadays most have disappeared. Southern Railway No.764 emerged from the works of the North British Locomotive Company, Glasgow in May 1925 gaining the appellation, along with sisters Nos.763 to 792, of the 'Scotch Arthurs'. No.30764 was withdrawn in July 1961 and its British Railways shed allocations were: Stewarts Lane; June 1955 Eastleigh; July 1955 Bournemouth; September 1960 Salisbury; October 1960 Bournemouth.

Upon the death of his father, Lot of Orkney, Sir Gawain became head of the Orkney clan, which included his brothers Agravain, Gaheris and Gareth, all of whom died, by accident, at Sir Lancelot's hands. Gawain thus became the mortal enemy of his once best friend and in the inevitable fight Gawain was mortally wounded, but before dying he forgave the grieving Lancelot. *(BLP - S59)*

An unidentified but rebuilt 'Battle of Britain' Pacific waits under the magnificent signal gantry that stood at the west end of Basingstoke station, with an express for Southampton, September 1964. In all, sixty of the one hundred and ten 'West Country' and 'Battle of Britain' light Pacifics were rebuilt, starting with No.34005 BARNSTAPLE, in June 1957, and concluding with No.34104 BERE ALSTON, in May 1961. Of that sixty, only seventeen were 'Battle of Britain' class engines. Today, some twenty Bulleid Light Pacifics are preserved around Britain, ten of each in their original and rebuilt forms. (BLP - S24)

'King Arthur' No.30448 SIR TRISTRAM is seen at Exmouth Junction engine shed in May 1959 after working down from Salisbury with a local train. First of a batch of ten locomotives which Maunsell classed as 'G14 rebuilds', they were in fact new construction with 'watercart' tenders from withdrawn Drummond Class G14s. SIR TRISTRAM spent all his British Railways days allocated to 72B Salisbury shed before withdrawal in August 1960.

According to Le Morte d'Artur, Sir Tristram was the son of Meliodas, King of Lyonesse and champion to his uncle, King Mark of Cornwall. As that champion Tristram was sent to Ireland to escort the Lady Iseult to be married to Mark, but instead the pair fell in love and fled. It is said that Mark had his revenge by stabbing Tristram in the back as he was playing his harp for Iseult. *(BLP - S25)*

Still carrying the old British Railways emblem, Class E4 0-6-2T No.32577 sits in the yard of Brighton shed in April 1958. This class of engines was a larger wheeled development, by Billinton, of Stroudley's E3 class 0-6-2T which, though designed for goods work, had put in good performances with passenger trains. Seventy-five locomotives of Class E4 were built, with four later being rebuilt by Marsh to Class E4X. As normal with London Brighton & South Coast engines, all were named at building. LB&SCR 577 came out of Brighton works in June 1903, named BLACKSTONE. Numbered 2577 by the Southern Railway and 32577 by BR, the locomotive was finally withdrawn in October 1959. She spent her entire British Railways career working from 75A Brighton shed. *(BLP - S56)*

Approaching Honiton tunnel with a Down express in May 1959, 'BB' 34075 264 SQUADRON, is having to work hard, as it nears the end of almost six miles of 1 in 80 gradient! Emerging from Brighton works on 9th June 1948, 34075 was a fairly early Bulleid Light Pacific casualty, being officially recorded as withdrawn by the Western Region in April 1964. The locomotive was seen at Bird's yard, Bridgend on 10th July 1965, but was scrapped sometime during the following year. British Railways shed allocations: Dover; September 1950 Stewarts Lane; January 1951 Dover; May 1952 Ramsgate; September 1957 Exmouth Junction.

A World War I seaplane squadron, 264 was disbanded on 1st March 1919 and reformed on 30th October 1939, at Sutton Bridge, equipped with the Boulton-Paul Defiant 4-gun turret fighter. Finding to their great cost that the Defiant was unsuitable for day fighter work, the squadron switched to night fighting at the end of August 1940. 264 Squadron's Battle of Britain bases were Duxford and Kirton-in-Lindsey. *(BLP - S54)*

Un-rebuilt 'West Country' Pacific 34038 LYNTON climbs Honiton bank with an Exeter to Salisbury local train, in May 1959. The light train would have presented the 4-6-2 with no problem on the nearly five miles at around 1 in 80/90 of the westbound climb to the summit at Honiton tunnel. As Southern Railway No.21C138, the Pacific entered traffic on 5th September 1946 and worked just under twenty years, being withdrawn, still in original form, on 12th June 1966 after running 819,984 miles; she was cut up at Cashmore's, Newport some three months later. British Railways shed allocations: Brighton; April 1951 Plymouth Friary; December 1957 Exmouth Junction; November 1960 Brighton; October 1961 Eastleigh; January 1965 Nine Elms. *(BLP - S1)*

(opposite) Class H 0-4-4T No.31278 stands at Westerham station with a branch train for Dunton Green, in May 1960. This particular locomotive was considered a bit of a rarity because it was one of only three members of the class that had a straight sided bunker; it is not known why a few of the H class were made so. At the time the picture was taken 31278 was allocated to 75F Tunbridge Wells West shed, so what it was doing at Westerham, when working of that branch was normally a Tonbridge depot duty, is open to conjecture. Whatever, No.31278 was withdrawn from service in September 1962; BR shed allocations: Bricklayers Arms; April 1951 Ashford; May 1953 Dover; April 1956 Tunbridge Wells West. Some interesting asides about these 0-4-4Ts are that at first only sixty-four were constructed, but when Maunsell took over as Locomotive Superintendent he found that the kits of parts for the other two engines had been kept, presumably as a source of spares. On his orders the last two engines were then erected - in 1915, nine years after the sixty-fourth engine had been delivered. Regarding design features, they had unique pagoda-like cab roofs and some parts were interchangeable with the Class C 0-6-0 goods engines; and lastly, such was their usefulness that during World War Two, the LMS borrowed three locomotives for service in Scotland - Nos.1177 and 1184 stationed at Forfar, with No.1259 at Aberdeen. Besides these three, the LMS also had two B1's; six D1's; nine F1's; five K10's; ten S11's; six T1's, and one T9. These particular engines worked at places ranging from Templecombe to Inverness and Bristol to Peterborough. *(BLP - S191)*

N Class 2-6-0 No.31847 is here seen leaving Exeter (St. Davids) with a Down local train, for North Devon, in May 1961. Maunsell's first N class engine came out of Ashford works in July 1917 and Southern aficionados remain uncomfortably aware that the design was heavily influenced by Great Western thinking, because Maunsell's assistant, Harry Holcroft, was working at Ashford, ex-Swindon works! The footplatemen nicknamed the engines 'Woolworths' but in reality the N class proved a very viable locomotive for employment anywhere on the Southern Railway on duties ranging from pick-up goods to semi-fast passenger. The Ns' free steaming capability was especially appreciated during the heavy traffic of the Second World War and all came into the BR sphere. No.31847 was withdrawn in September 1963, having spent all its' British Railways' career working from 72A (83D) Exmouth Junction. *(BLP - S121)*

Nearing the summit of the 1 in 37 gradient from Exeter (St. Davids), 'Battle of Britain' No.34078 222 SQUADRON, enters Exeter (Central) station with an Up passenger train, in April 1963. Always a problem to operate, the London & South Western, Southern, and British Railways all had to employ banking engines to assist most trains up that severe slope, usually from a standing start; the sounds of such workings are not easily forgotten! No.34078 came into traffic on 21st July 1948 and remained in original condition until withdrawn by the Western Region in September 1964. Scrapping took place at Bird's Morriston. BR shed allocations: Ramsgate; June 1959 Bricklayers Arms; January 1961 Exmouth Junction.

222 Squadron formed at Duxford on 5th October 1939 equipped with Blenheims, for shipping protection duties. In March 1940 it re-equipped with Spitfires as a day fighter unit and served during the Battle of Britain at Kirton-in-Lindsey and Hornchurch airfields. *(BLP - S100)*

'Battle of Britain' Pacific No.34054 LORD BEAVERBROOK nears Farnborough with a Down local train for Salisbury, in September 1963, only fifteen months before the engine was withdrawn, with 737,443 miles run. British Railways shed allocations: Nine Elms; March 1951 Exmouth Junction; May 1952 Salisbury; October 1963 Exmouth Junction. Scrapped at Bird's Bynea yard in March 1965.

The engine was named in honour of the Canadian-born William Maxwell Aitkin, who moved to Britain and became a Conservative MP and newspaper magnate. He held several Ministerial positions in Winston Churchill's wartime government, the most crucial being Minister for Aircraft Production, 1940-41. Lord Beaverbrook died in 1964. *(BLP - S117)*

With steam to spare rebuilt 'West Country' No.34046 BRAUNTON leaves Farnborough cutting with an Up express in September 1963. White's *Devonshire Directory* (1850), describes Braunton thus: "…Braunton, the large ancient village which gives name to this Hundred and Petty Sessional Division, is situated on the banks of a rivulet about 2 miles from the sea coast and the Taw estuary, and 5 miles W.N.W. of Barnstaple. Its extensive parish contains 2274 inhabitants, and 9951 acres of land, extending to the sea coast and the estuary of the Taw, and including the scattered hamlets of Saunton, Lobb, Nethercott, Knoll, Winsham, Halsinger, Pippacot, and Boode..." In later years the area was to become a very popular holiday resort, because of the superb sandy beaches thereabouts. No.34046 entered service on 14th November 1946 and was rebuilt in February 1959 only to be withdrawn just over six year later on 10th October 1965; she was to be one of the twenty Light Pacifics preserved and today is at the West Somerset Railway. British Railways shed allocations: Exmouth Junction; April 1951 Salisbury; June 1951 Brighton; February 1959 Bournemouth. *(BLP - S104)*

Rebuilt 'Battle of Britain' No.34059 SIR ARCHIBALD SINCLAIR, runs 'light engine' from the east, towards Basingstoke station in September 1964; Mr Pirt did not advance a reason for this working. As noted elsewhere No.34059 was constructed in 1947. The engine ran for 569,583 miles before being rebuilt in early 1960, and was withdrawn on 29th May 1966 after running a further 307,524 miles. Today the Pacific is preserved on the Bluebell Railway. British Railways shed allocations: Nine Elms; March 1951 Exmouth Junction; October 1955 Salisbury. *(BLP - S10)*

Having just worked a Down express from London, 'WC' 34002 SALISBURY waits to enter Exmouth Junction engine shed, in May 1961. The Southern Railway was a big user of concrete for all forms of structure - in fact a large concrete depot for making all kinds of items stood only yards away from this engine shed. The form of construction, using concrete blocks for the shed walls may easily be seen, together with the 'northlight' roof pattern which, when built using more traditional materials, had proved to be very vulnerable and therefore maintenance-intensive. Not so with concrete! Of note in the picture is the small water tank, set very high, such a phenomenon was unique in British engine shed history. At one time atop the tank was the post and arm of a semaphore signal which was used as part of the testing of footplatemen's eyesight - i.e. from a distance, was the arm "on" or "off" ? Again, a unique device for a locomotive depot. Also as alluded to in another caption, this large engine shed closed to steam in June 1965. *(BLP - S129)*

Class N1 2-6-0 No.31876 waits for its next duty at Tonbridge shed in May 1958. A development by Maunsell of his N class Mogul, only six N1 entered service, one (No.1822) in 1923, the others (Nos.1876 to 1880), in 1930. In place of the two cylinders of the N class, the N1 class had three, all using Walschaerts valve gear. In practice the three-cylinder engines did not show much of an improvement over their two-cylinder sisters, but the N1's smaller outside cylinders gave them route availability over the restricted Tonbridge to Hastings line, where they worked with some distinction. Such a small class was bound not to see a protracted withdrawal and in fact, all six engines were taken out of service en bloc, in November 1962. No.31876's British Railways shed allocations: Hither Green; May 1959 Tonbridge; June 1962 Stewarts Lane (depot re-coded 75D in June 1962 from 73A). *(BLP - S71)*

(opposite) Class L 4-4-0 No.31760 is seen beside the somewhat ramshackle coaling stage at Tonbridge shed, in May 1958. SE&CR No.760 was built by Beyer, Peacock & Co. in 1914 and like all the Class L, was popular with the footplatemen and a good performer. This is evidenced by the log of a run made on 3rd April 1956, when one of the Borsig-built engines, No.31776, hauled the 10.42 a.m. train from Ashford to Redhill. Departure from Ashford was six minutes late, with three coaches of 94 tons tare, 97 tons gross. Arrival at Tonbridge was on-time, No.31776 having covered the 26.6 miles in 42 minutes and six seconds, inclusive of stops at Pluckley, Headcorn, Staplehurst, Marden and Paddock Wood! Four separate maxima in excess of 60 m.p.h. were recorded with the highest speed, 68 m.p.h., being reached one mile before the Headcorn stop. Lively indeed! Main dimensions of the class were two cylinders, 19˚ by 26 inches, six foot eight inch driving wheels, a boiler pressure of 180 lbs per square inch and tractive effort, at 85% boiler pressure, of 18,910 lbs. Total weight was ninety eight tons and six hundredweight and the tender held five tons of coal and 3,500 gallons of water. No.31760 was withdrawn in July 1961; British Railways shed allocations: Tonbridge; May 1959 Nine Elms. *(BLP - S92)*

No.31500 and its' two-coach auto-train wait outside Tonbridge station for its' next working in June 1960. Such push-pull trains used to work along the main lines centred on Tonbridge and also over the local branch lines, all of which services ended in 1961. No.31500 ended her days working from Tonbridge shed in July of that year. BR shed allocations: Stewarts Lane; January 1951 Bricklayers Arms; November 1951 Faversham; February 1953 Ashford; September 1955 Ramsgate; May 1959 Nine Elms; November 1959 Tonbridge. The South Eastern Railway opened from Redhill to Tonbridge on 26th May 1842, the station remaining a railhead until extension to Paddock Wood and beyond on 25th September 1844. Almost exactly a year later - 20th September 1845 to be precise - the steeply graded line from Tonbridge to Tunbridge Wells opened and the last line to serve the town was that through Sevenoaks which came into use on 1st May 1868. In recent years of course Tonbridge took on greater importance when it became a major stopping point for the 'Eurostar' services between London and mainland Europe. That distinction seems set to diminish in the near future, however, when the new high speed line opens between Folkestone and London, St.Pancras. *(BLP - S177)*

Eastleigh engine shed, with N15 'King Arthur' class 4-6-0 No.30806, SIR GALLERON, standing in the sunshine. Mr Pirt notes the date as September 1963, but this surely is an error because 30806 was withdrawn from service in April 1961. Mr Pirt also notes that this engine, the last N15 to be built, in January 1927, was "…one of the rarer ex-South Eastern section 'Arthurs'…" but in fact the locomotive had been allocated to Eastleigh shed since May 1959. The sole British Railways shed allocation prior to Eastleigh was: Hither Green.

Sir Richard Malory's book on Arthurian legend, Le Morte d'Artur mentions Sir Galleron of Galway as being an injured knight who lent his armour to Sir Tristram, so that he might engage Sir Palomides in battle. *(BLP - S21)*

With the diamond-shaped builders plate of Dübs and Co., clearly visible on the centre splasher, '700' class 0-6-0 No.30368 is seen at Basingstoke shed in June 1960, with a Class U 2-6-0 alongside and what appears to be a Class H15 4-6-0 behind. The '700' class was saturated in its' original form, a situation reversed by Urie in 1919 with two experimental superheated locomotives and superheating was applied to the rest, after the Grouping, by Maunsell. This alteration alone required extending the smokebox and frames and raising the pitch of the boiler by no less than nine inches, but it gave rise to a rather useful stud of engines that, with one exception, lasted well beyond their sixtieth year of operation. No.30368 was built in 1897 and was withdrawn in December 1962, after spending all its' British Railways time working from Basingstoke (70D) shed. *(BLP - S183)*

Exmouth Junction engine shed forms the backdrop to' Merchant Navy' No.35013 BLUE FUNNEL, still carrying the (small) old British Railways emblem, passing with an Exeter-London express in May 1959. 21C13 was brought into use on 5th February 1945, being named Blue Funnel Line on the following 17th April by Mr L.Holt. For a reason yet to be determined, the nameplates were soon changed to Blue Funnel, with an added inscription in smaller letters, of the Latin Certum Pete Finum, which roughly translates to "Seek fineness (with) certainty"! When just under two years old the engine was involved in the working of fifteen coach, 500 ton test trains between Norwood Junction and Brighton, the outcome of which is uncertain. Rebuilding of the engine took place in May 1956 and despite coming close to withdrawal in February 1964, No.35013 was reprieved and lasted until the July 1967 end of steam on the Southern Region. During those final months BLUE FUNNEL acquired the reputation of being one of the more 'slippery' of her class with well recorded speeds of 104 m.p.h. on 28th April 1967 and no less than 106 m.p.h. on the 26th June - going out in a blaze of glory, to meet her end in the yard of Buttigiegs, Newport, just four months later. BR shed allocations: Nine Elms; March 1954 Exmouth Junction; August 1964 Bournemouth; October 1966 Weymouth; March 1967 Nine Elms.

The Blue Funnel shipping line was set up by Alfred Holt in 1866 with the first three ships, Agamemnon, Ajax and Achilles, being used on the Liverpool-China run. The company's last ship, Myrmidon, entered service in 1980 (being built in the same Greenock yard as the first three, named above), by 1986 Blue Funnel was no more. *(BLP - S53)*

'West Country' Class No.34002 SALISBURY coasts through Pokesdown with a Down express in August 1965. The line through Pokesdown opened on 14th March 1870 when rails were extended from Christchurch to Bournemouth East. The first station on the site seen here was actually called Boscombe, opening 1st July 1886, and renamed Pokesdown (Boscombe) on 1st October 1891. The next renaming came on 1st July 1897, when the station became simply Pokesdown - this lasting until 1930 when it became Pokesdown for eastern Bournemouth. Finally, British Railways renamed the station Pokesdown again! Pacific 34002 was built in June 1945, changing its number from 21C102, to 34002, in October 1948. Never rebuilt, the engine ran 1,003,613 miles before withdrawal in April 1967, to be scrapped at Cashmore's Newport, six months later. BR shed allocations: Exmouth Junction; August 1964 Eastleigh, January 1965 Nine Elms. *(BLP - S48)*

A classic 'engine on shed' picture as, with drain cocks hissing, 35029 ELLERMAN LINES moves off Exmouth Junction depot in May 1959. One of the last two 'Merchant Navy' Class locomotives to be rebuilt, in September 1959, ELLERMAN LINES also still carries the old British Railways 'Lion & Wheel' emblem, some three years after its replacement was introduced. 35029 came into service on 19th February 1949, was named on 1st March 1951 and ran until withdrawal in September 1966, with the lowest total of miles run in service of the entire 'MN' Class - 748,343. The engine went to Woodham's at Barry in May 1967 and was retrieved seven years later to win fame as being the sectioned steam locomotive displayed at the National Railway Museum, York. BR shed allocations: Dover; June 1955 Nine Elms; August 1964 Weymouth.

The Ellerman Lines Company was formed in Liverpool in 1892, by purchase of a fleet of twenty-two ships from the executors of Frederick Leyland. By 1939 it was one of the largest merchant shipping companies of the world with 105 vessels, of which no fewer than sixty were lost during World War 2. The fleet had been rebuilt to ninety-four ships by 1953, but in 2002 the company was declared 'dormant'. *(BLP - S52)*

The last of her graceful line! Britain's one and only remaining working Atlantic type, Class H2 No.32424 BEACHY HEAD, is seen in Brighton shed yard on her last working day in April 1958. This 4-4-2 class and its immediate predecessor Atlantic type, the H1, were designed by Marsh who, prior to coming to the London Brighton & South Coast Railway, had been assistant to H.A.Ivatt at the Great Northern Railway's works at Doncaster. It can be no surprise therefore, that the Marsh Atlantics bore a very strong resemblance to Ivatt's large GNR 4-4-2 design. LB&SCR No.424 came from Brighton works in September 1911 and was withdrawn - officially - during the period 8th May to 6th June 1958. British Railways shed allocations: Newhaven; April 1951 Brighton. Sadly, no British Atlantic of any type was preserved, but miraculously, a few years ago, an ex-Ivatt Large Atlantic boiler was discovered and it today forms the centrepiece of a scheme by the Bluebell Railway, to build a replica Marsh 4-4-2. *(BLP - S61)*

Fresh from a General overhaul at Ashford works, Class E4 No.32484 sparkles in lined-out black livery at Ashford shed, in May 1958. Built at Brighton in May 1899, as London Brighton & South Coast Railway No.484 HACKBRIDGE, the 0-6-2T was to survive, despite the major overhaul, only until withdrawal in September 1960. The E4 class can be considered to have been very successful for its designed purpose of handling heavy suburban traffic, but their usefulness in all types of duty was epitomised by twelve of the engines being sent to France between 1917 and 1919 and one being tried out on the Isle of Wight. All except one engine of the class of seventy-five came into British Railways use, with the last being withdrawn in June 1963. No.32484's BR shed allocations were: Three Bridges; November 1954 Norwood Junction; January 1955 Three Bridges; September 1955 Brighton. *(BLP - S60)*

Resplendent in ex-works condition, after a 'Light Intermediate' overhaul, rebuilt 'BB' No.34052 LORD DOWDING rests in the yard of Eastleigh shed in April 1960. As No.21C152 the Pacific entered traffic on New Year's Eve 1946 and was named by Lord Dowding at Waterloo station on 11th September 1947 (he also named 21C151 WINSTON CHURCHILL on the same occasion). The engine was rebuilt in September 1958 and was withdrawn on 9th July 1967, with a total of 936,502 miles run. British Railways shed allocations: Nine Elms; March 1951 Exmouth Junction; June 1951 Salisbury.

Hugh Caswall Tremenheere Dowding was born in Moffat in 1882 and rose to become Commander-in-Chief of RAF Fighter Command between July 1936 and November 1940. His pivotal role in preparing his force for, and leading it during, the Battle of Britain, have been compared to Drake's and Nelson's feats in saving Britain at a time of great danger. Lord Hugh Dowding died in 1970. *(BLP - S159)*

Robertsbridge station in April 1958 with Class A1X 0-6-0T No.32646 waiting with a special train for the Kent & East Sussex Railway to Tenterden, while a 'Schools' Class 4-4-0 approaches at speed, with a train from London to Hastings. The history of No.32646 has been told earlier so we shall not dwell further upon it. However, the lines themselves are worthy of study. The South Eastern Railway opened the 15˘ miles from Tunbridge Wells to Robertsbridge on 1st September 1851, the latter remaining a temporary railhead until the six mile extension to Battle, through Mountfield tunnel was made on 1st January 1852. Extension on from Battle, another six miles, to Bopeep came one month later and at last ended a rate cutting war between the SER and London Brighton & South Coast Railway for traffic to Hastings. A fifty-fifty division of receipts was afterwards agreed between the two companies. Goods traffic between the SER and K&ESLR began with opening of the latter, on 29th March 1900. The SER had built a short spur to meet with the K&ESLR and the Light Railway's passenger trains began running into Robertsbridge station on 2nd April 1900 - traffic that would cease on 4th January 1954, with goods continuing for a further seven and a half years. Sadly, the trains of the re-opened K&ESR are unlikely to run once again into Robertsbridge because of a 1973 agreement between the railway and the then Minister of Transport, to drop proposals for re-opening between Bodiam and Robertsbridge, which would entail three level crossing of busy main roads. Said agreement was struck to avoid what remained of the line at that time, from being demolished. *(BLP - S70)*

30917 ARDINGLY, is seen at Tonbridge shed in May 1958, wearing the lined black livery that was first applied to the 'Schools' Class by British Railways. Given the class's fine reputation, this colour scheme was not popular and all members later received the BR Green livery. No.30917 carries the multiple blastpipe chimney that was applied by Bulleid to some of the class, but this reportedly made no visible improvement to these engines' already good performance. AS Southern Railway No.917, the 4-4-0 emerged from Eastleigh in May 1933 and was withdrawn in November 1962. BR shed allocations: Ramsgate; May 1959 Nine Elms; June 1959 Brighton.
The Anglican Ardingly College was founded in 1858 and today is a co-educational school for 400 pupils. It also now has been expanded by associated pre-Preparatory and Junior schools. *(BLP - S57)*

Mr Pirt's note for this picture reads "…30913 CHRIST'S HOSPITAL ready for eastbound action at Basingstoke shed, March 1960…" Action is a good word for association with the lively 'Schools', as evidenced by a performance log from 3rd April 1956. This was when No.30934 ST. LAWRENCE, hauling the 9.15 a.m. Charing Cross to Ramsgate, left Tonbridge eleven minutes late, with eleven coaches of 366 tons tare, 395 tons full, on the thirty-one minute schedule to Ashford, 26.6 miles away. The 19.2 miles from Paddock Wood to Chart Siding was run at an average speed of 67.2 m.p.h. with a maximum of 72 m.p.h. at Staplehurst and a very good 64 m.p.h. at the end of the long rise to Chart Siding. Start to stop time to Ashford was exactly 28 minutes, therefore arriving eight minutes late. No.30913 emerged from Eastleigh in September 1932 and was withdrawn in February 1962. British Railways shed allocations: Ramsgate; May 1959 Nine Elms.
Edward VI granted The Palace of Bridewell and his lands of the Savoy to create three Royal Hospitals, of which Christ's was one, for the education of poor children. The first boys and girls entered the School in Newgate in 1552 relocating to a purpose built site at Horsham in 1897. Today the school provides co-education to over 800 full boarding pupils from 13 to 18 years of age. *(BLP - S87)*

'King Arthur' 4-6-0 No.30788 SIR URRE OF THE MOUNT, waits his next duty at Basingstoke engine shed in June 1960. Another of the so-called 'Scotch Arthurs', No.788 was built by the NBL Co. in September 1925 and was withdrawn in February 1962. British Railways shed allocations: Nine Elms; January 1951 Eastleigh.

The Arthurian knight Sir Urre of the Mount was reputedly a Hungarian who killed a Spanish knight, Sir Alphegus, in a tournament. Alphegus's mother was a witch and she cursed Sir Urre with seven wounds that would never heal until the greatest knight in the world "searched" them. Eventually ending up in the Court of King Arthur, it is said that 110 of the knights of the Round Table searched Sir Urre's wounds, to no avail. Only when Sir Lancelot carried out his search was Sir Urre cured. He was then invited to stay on as a knight of the Round Table. *(BLP - S161)*

Seventy four locomotives of the 'King Arthur' class were built, but only one survived into preservation in the National Collection - No.30777 SIR LAMIEL. That survivor is viewed here, sidelined at the rear of Basingstoke engine shed in June 1960. That was sixteen months prior to withdrawal and subsequent storage at a number of locations, before being restored to working order in the 1980's - currently No.30777 is not in running condition. Built in June 1925, No.30777's British Railways shed allocations were: Nine Elms; June 1951 Stewarts Lane; September 1951 Dover; May 1959 Feltham; September 1960 Basingstoke.

Malory's Le Morte d'Artur mentions Sir Lamiel in Book 19, Chapter 11, as one of the 110 knights who "searched" the wounds of Sir Urre of the Mount. The book also notes that Sir Lamiel came from Cardiff and that he was "...a great lover..."! *(BLP - S182)*

'West Country' No.34018 AXMINSTER at work and at rest. In the picture opposite the Pacific is seen leaving Basingstoke with a Down Bournemouth line express, in September 1963. *(above)* Flanked by a BR Standard and a 'Lord Nelson', 34018 rests between duties in the yard at Eastleigh shed, in April 1960. As No.21C118, this engine entered service a week before Christmas 1945 and ran 547,303 miles before rebuilding in September 1958. In her new form No.34018 covered a further 427,014 miles before being withdrawn on the last day of Southern Region steam, 9th July 1967. After a period in store, the Pacific was moved to Cashmore's Newport, where scrapping occurred in April 1968. British Railways shed allocations: Exmouth Junction; March 1951 Nine Elms; December 1963 Eastleigh; June 1966 Nine Elms. *(BLP - S111 & S158)*

A 'Greyhound' at rest, at Padstow, in July 1957; T9 No.30708 was just five months from withdrawal and eventual scrapping. Mr Drummond's highly successful design of 4-4-0 was introduced in 1899, with two batches being built, one by Nine Elms works, the other by Dübs & Co. of Glasgow. No.708, as she was numbered when built, was part of the Dubs batch that introduced cross water tubes in the fireboxes, which increased the heating surface and in fact, henceforth became the standard for all future Drummond passenger engines. The T9s will always be associated with the 8-wheel 'watercart' tender as seen here, but when built the 1899 batches had 6-wheel tenders and in fact, various members of the class were fitted with them over the years, when allocated to the Southern Railway's Central Section. Note also the separate 'outboard' splasher which accommodated the rod throw; the next batch of fifteen engines built at Nine Elms during 1900-01, differed in having a wider splasher that housed the rods and wheels together. No.30708's BR shed allocations: Exmouth Junction; November 1950 Bournemouth; November 1951 Basingstoke; September 1952 Exmouth Junction. *(BLP - S11)*

'West Country' No.34094 MORTHOE fast approaches Basingstoke station with an Up express in June 1960. This locomotive had a somewhat short life, being put into traffic in October 1949, only to be withdrawn in August 1964 - a working life of less than fifteen years and with only 672,346 miles run. Singularly unlucky then, because although 34094 was consigned to Woodham's yard at Barry, she was not saved like many of her sisters, but became one of the few locomotives actually cut up there, in November 1964! British Railways shed allocations: Bournemouth; February 1958 Nine Elms. *(BLP - S199)*

Another S15 caught on camera in Basingstoke Down yard at the earlier date of June 1960, was also awaiting departure with a fitted freight for Salisbury. Redhill based No.30836 was a somewhat grubbier specimen and was fitted with a small six-wheel tender. The first Eastleigh-built batch (1927) included engines for services on the Southern Railway's Eastern and Central sections so some were fitted with six wheeled tenders for use where there were small turntables. Over time, tenders were changed around within the class and also exchanged with 'King Arthurs', the 'Schools' (which received their six-wheeled tenders) and with the 'Lord Nelson' class. Originally built, like the 'King Arthurs', without smoke deflectors, these were eventually fitted to the first two batches in the mid-1930s. No.30836 entered service in 1936 and was withdrawn in June 1964. British Railways shed allocations: Feltham; July 1951 Redhill; June 1963 Feltham. *(BLP - S114)*

With a rake of ex-London Midland and Scottish Railway coaching stock, 'West Country' No.34047 CALLINGTON, takes the Reading line out of Basingstoke with a Bournemouth to Sheffield service, in September 1964. In the background can be seen the former Great Western Railway goods shed, a reminder of the time when that railway had its own passenger and goods stations in the town. The Pacific came into service on 23rd November 1946 and was rebuilt in October 1958, having run some 513,822 miles. Withdrawal from service occurred on 25th June 1967 after a further 332,169 miles had been covered; scrapping was at Buttigieg's yard, Newport some 6 or 7 months later. British Railways shed allocations: Exmouth Junction; April 1951 Salisbury; June 1951 Brighton; September 1958 Nine Elms; May 1959 Bournemouth. *(BLP - S150)*

Lowly duty for 35004 CUNARD WHITE STAR, passing Basingstoke engine shed as she departs with a Down local train for the West of England line in September 1963. Delivered to service on 29th October 1941, the locomotive was named by Sir P.E.Bates, Chairman of Cunard White Star, on 1st January 1942 - the naming took place, unusually, at London's Charing Cross station. The engine suffered the indignity of being shot at by the Luftwaffe in November 1942; the attack took place near Whimple, but thankfully no damage was done. Black livery was applied to 21C4 in July 1943 with reversion to Malachite green in April 1946, six months before the engine was appropriately used for hauling a boat train to Southampton, for the first passenger sailing of the liner Queen Elizabeth. No.35004 was rebuilt in July 1958 and ran until 28th October 1965 when the engine severely slipped while hauling a Bournemouth-Waterloo express. The slip buckled the coupling rods causing the engine to be declared a 'failure' but although the damage was in no way serious, funds were not made available for repairs, so 35004 was withdrawn after running 1,131,417 miles. Storage at Eastleigh shed lasted until February 1966 when she was scrapped on site by Messrs. Cohens. BR shed allocations: Exmouth Junction; March 1957 Salisbury; August 1964 Bournemouth.

Arguably the world's most famous shipping line, Cunard White Star did not come into being until 10th May 1934 when amalgamation of the two North Atlantic arch-rivals - i.e. Cunard and White Star Line - was brought about by Government insistence as part of a financial package to complete the building of the 81,000 ton Queen Mary. All possible former White Star assets were disposed of as quickly as possible and eventually just the name Cunard remained, with world famous ships still plying the seas today. *(BLP - S97)*

Ex-South Eastern & Chatham Railway Class H No.31305 waits in the sunshine at Tonbridge shed, for its' next duty, in June 1960, when the class was being threatened with large-scale withdrawal from service. The Class H had been a feature at Tonbridge shed for some years, especially for working the branch lines to Hawkhurst and Westerham and push-pull services along the stations of the main lines radiating from Tonbridge. Quite what this particular locomotive was doing at Tonbridge is unclear because at the time, it was officially allocated to Bricklayers Arms depot in south London. Most probably it was on loan, or there had been an un-recorded transfer? At this point in time it is difficult to know what might have gone on, "on the quiet" as it were! No.31305 was withdrawn from service in November 1962 and its BR shed allocations were: Ashford; June 1951 Faversham; June 1952 Gillingham; July 1953 Faversham; September 1955 Bricklayers Arms; June 1962 Stewarts Lane. Tonbridge engine shed was indeed, a venerable depot. The first three-road dead-end building was opened by the South Eastern Railway on 26th May 1842. By 1880 another three-road section had been added, adjoining the first and slightly en echelon to it; the first section had also been made a 'through' building. These brick, built, pitched roof structures came into British Railways ownership, but in poor condition, so they were comprehensively re-roofed in concrete with brick end screens, in 1952. The depot officially closed to steam on the 17th June 1962, but actually remained in use for servicing visiting steam locomotives until January 1965. Thereafter diesels used the shed until it was demolished, leaving just the stabling roads and one wall, which had the shed offices attached. When the site ceased to be used for stabling motive power is unknown. *(BLP - S63)*

'Merchant Navy' 4-6-2 No.35008 ORIENT LINE, hurries the Down *BOURNEMOUTH BELLE* Pullman train through Basingstoke in September 1964; just glimpsed is the Bulleid designed restaurant car in the formation of a passing Up express. The story of 35008 is told elsewhere in this book so there is little to add here. However, Basingstoke itself had an interesting history with the London & Southampton Railway opening from its former railhead at Shapley Heath (Winchfield), on 10th June 1839. Basingstoke remained a railhead, complete with a small engine shed, until the rails were extended to Winchester on 11th May 1840, thereby completing the London & Southampton's route. Next to arrive was the broad gauge Berks & Hants Railway from Reading, in reality a Great Western Railway sponsored line. The Berks & Hants had a separate station adjoining that of the LSWR, this remaining in use until closure on 1st January 1932, after which GWR trains ran into the Southern Railway station. The Berks & Hants initially provided itself with a simple locomotive servicing facility at Basingstoke, but in 1850 a two-road engine shed was provided with the unusual construction of one side wall in wood, the other in brick (with an eye on possible future expansion perhaps?), that was closed by British Railways in November 1950. On the last day of the GWR's independent existence, three Pannier tanks were out-stationed from Reading shed: Nos.4649, 4661 and 4670. Thereafter, any Western Region locomotive requiring fuel or attention went to the Southern Region shed (70D). The last development was the opening of the Basingstoke & Alton Light Railway, which never turned a profit and was closed on 1st January 1917. However, the Southern Railway was coerced into re-opening the line on 18th August 1924, but it was closed again, to passengers, on 12th September 1932 and goods, on 1st June 1936. Before it passed totally into history though, the Basingstoke & Alton won classic fame by being used for the Will Hay film, *"Oh, Mr. Porter"*. (BLP - S189)